Illustrated by El Davo

To Tammy.
For your unwavering trust in me.
I love you. x

David Robertson

This book is so good that I want to keep putting it down. Todd Eden has succeeded in creating a book on personal development that is genuinely and profoundly thought-provoking. Right from the start, the questions, and exercises grabbed my attention and had me putting the book down to think and reflect. I have always a very occasional journaler, but since reading Own Life I have been loving finding quiet moments throughout the day to focus on the bigger questions. The book is both practical and energising. It helps you to reflect on what really matters to you, but then it helps you to put in place practical and actionable strategies to help you take control of your life. I love it.

Todd has taught thousands of delegates around the world, and after completing the course, each one is asked, 'What will you do differently now?'

Here follows a selection of their responses, which all start with

"I will…"

'… achieve my goals whatever it may take.' [Charidimos V]
'… be much more confident.' [Hadra A]
'… be more confident talking to new people.' [Elizabeth G]
'… be more grateful about being myself.' [Mohamad A]
'… be a better version of myself.' [Nicole E]
'… believe in myself.' [Maddi M]
'… change.' [Alex M]
'… achieve my potential.' [Abdulla R]
'… be more productive.' [Fahmid C]
'… feel comfortable being myself to others.' [Elissar B]
'… be more resilient to the voices in my head.' [Natasha J]
'… be more aware of the potential that I have.' [Emine O]
'… start improving my habits and focus on priorities.' [Marta M]
'… be more interactive with others.' [Dongho L]
'… manage my problems well.' [Umar T]
'… be more open.' [Marta O]
'… handle setbacks better.' [Rosemary C]
'… stop coming up with excuses.' [Javor G]
'… be more positive.' [Mathilda C]
'… be more motivated to achieve my goals.' [Iva K]
'… strive to better my self-discipline.' [Sean M]
'… step out of my comfort zone.' [Margherita C]
'… be more organized.' [Abdul R]
'… have more purpose in everything I do.' [Luksa K]

'... be more committed towards my goals.' [Mohamed A]

'... be more productive.' [Sharon S]

'... face my fears.' [Tanu C]

'... be more confident in myself.' [Madalina M]

'... have purpose in my actions.' [Louise M]

'... face the tasks that I avoid because of fear.' [James W]

'... step out of my comfort zone.' [Daniela B]

'... start changing unhealthy habits.' [Augustin L]

'... set goals for myself.' [Nilay S]

'... pursue my goals.' [Jeremiah U]

'... implement mindfulness.' [Lauren C]

'... be an active listener.' [Anira B]

'... set my goals.' [Imani S]

'... know myself better.' [Abhishek B]

'... not be afraid to share my thoughts with others.' [Disha S]

'... make the most of what I have.' [Tiffany D]

'... be more authentic.' [Ellarene C]

'... accept myself.' [Alice V]

'... apply for jobs I was unsure about.' [Marco A]

'... believe in my ability.' [Hannah S]

'... be more confident in myself.' [Amy F]

'... appreciate different opinions.' [Ana M]

'... work harder towards my goals.' [Andres G]

'... face my future strong.' [Arjunan R]

'... commit with purpose.' [Camilo R]

'... push myself to leave my comfort zone.' [Daniel C]

'... keep improving myself.' [Emmanuel O]

'... control my inner voice.' [Hiren T]

'... be a better leader.' [Ieva G]

'... adopt mindfulness and talk to strangers.' [James T]

'... feel more confident around people.' [Jessica F]

'... be more self-aware.' [Kabilas P]

'... feel more confident to apply for certain jobs.' [Katherine H]

'... put myself in the shoes of others more often.' [Kilian B]

'... take responsibility for my life.' [Lanja R]

'... take risks.' [Lauren M]

'... get out of my comfort zone.' [Madhumitha K]

'... listen more.' [Michal C]

'... be more confident.' [Nantia B]

'... have more confidence in myself.' [Polly S]

'... be more mindful.' [Rosie G]

'... be more ready to take the lead.' [Samuel S]

'... be more introspective.' [Sian W]

'... take better care of my health.' [Sushma S]

'... always say positive things about myself.' [Toyyibat B]

'... be more resilient.' [Yakubu S]

'... be willing to step out of my comfort zone.' [Sabrina C]

'... continue to be me.' [Samantha C]

'... make a difference.' [Debbie F]

'... believe in myself more.' [Manvinder D]

'... express myself better.' [Hasit G]

'... be kinder to myself.' [Jad J]

'... trust other people more.' [Ashley A]

'... stop trying to solve other people's problems.' [Brandon M]

'... be more understanding.' [Noi B]

By the end of this book, what will you be doing?

CONTENTS

HOW TO DEVELOP POSITIVE RELATIONSHIPS

The quality of your relationships largely determines the quality of your life. Your emotional state is closely related to the nature of your relationships with the people you spend the most time with. If they are nurturing and respectful, you experience satisfaction, self-confidence and happiness. If they are critical and disrespectful, you experience sadness and low self-esteem.

William James says, 'the deepest principle in human nature is the craving to be appreciated', and Dale Carnegie[1] adds 'the rare individual who can honestly satisfy this heart hunger will hold people in the palm of his hand'.

Whilst you can't control another person, you can choose how you show up in a relationship and it is this skill that you'll be developing over the course of this book. By the end, my wish is that you have shifted your mindset and begun to change some behaviours so that you enjoy more fulfilling relationships with everyone in your life. Specifically, I'd like you to:

- Nurture those relationships that bring you most emotional satisfaction.
- Deepen the way you listen with an open heart.
- Treat conflict as a requirement for seeing the world afresh.
- Give well thought through feedback if you are hurt by others.
- Readdress imbalance in relationships by seeking to hold the adult position.
- Dive into the four dimensions of trust to build positive relationships.
- Manage your internal state and crack a smile at every opportunity.
- Honour the presence of other people by being fully present with them.

Over the next few weeks, I'll show you how to achieve all this, and I'm genuinely excited for you. Let's dial up your life satisfaction!

HOW TO OWN LIFE

This may not be your first book from the Own Life Collection, so you'll recognise this guidance, and if you're new to the series, then welcome! ;-)

To truly Own Life takes some time, so be patient with the book and yourself. Give the concepts space to breathe, and your experiments the necessary time to achieve their desired results. In every book in the collection, you'll be learning how to live with greater self-confidence and how to set your path to own your future.

Unlike many self-help books, we are not attempting to turn you into someone new, to add another mask, which is exhausting to live up to. You will always be you, and we want you to be ALL of you, ALL of the time.

When you allow yourself, being you is so easy, and nobody else does it better!

This is your life journey, and this is your book. At the moment the book in your hand looks like anybody else's, but shortly you'll start to add your own notes, in your own way, with your unique handwriting, and instantly this book is like no other on the planet.

Your life too is in your hands. How much you own it depends on how much you invest in it. In a moment you'll be answering a set of questions which will put you on the path to becoming more self-aware, and it's through the lens of 'yourself' that we'll do great work together. Yes, there are models and theories, lots of them in fact, but it's how you relate to them that matters – so when there's a pause in the text and a question for you to ponder, really do it.

Throughout the book, you'll see sections titled 'Reflect & Write'. This is your invitation to do just that. Take some quiet time to consider each of the questions, allow your thoughts and feelings to emerge, and then crystalize them by putting pen to paper. The act of writing down your thoughts helps them settle in your mind and brings a comforting level of clarity. I don't think of you as readers, I think of you as participants, so read this book with a pen in your hand.

The insights you gain about yourself can be revelatory yet remain merely interesting. To shift the dial of your life requires action, and throughout the book you'll be invited to conduct small experiments to tweak your ingrained behaviours.

From time to time you may have a question that you need some help with; or maybe you'd like to connect with others who are struggling with similar issues; or you'd like to share a moment of enlightenment, or a piece of advice; or be inspired by other people's Own Life journey. For any of this, head to www.ownlife.me/connect and we'll take this journey together.

HOW'S IT ALL GOING?

Before we start, it's helpful to get a baseline on how things are really going for you. We're starting with a wide lens to check-in on how fully you are Owning Life as a whole. We do this to put *OWNING LIFE WITH TRUST* into context and to notice which other facets of life you might be able to draw strengths from, or which need additional support so they don't trip you up.

Put a date on the page, and if you've completed this task in previous books in the Own Life collection, do this again first before reading your notes from last time.

Reflect & Write: You've lived on this planet for quite some time now. How's it going? How is life turning out for you? On this occasion you'll notice that I give you a relatively small box to write in. We just want to get an overall impression at this stage.

Perhaps you're thinking, 'It's a huge freakin' mess, and I don't know how to dig myself out.' Or maybe, 'Things are actually going pretty well, but is this it?' No matter how you respond to this question, if you want to get the most out of life, then this book will help you discover the authentic human you are and lay the foundations for living the life you are truly capable of living.

Consider the statements on the below with real honesty based on your experience of the last six months. Decide to what extent you agree or disagree with each of them, and colour in the corresponding box in the chart on the next page.

1. I know and accept myself for who I am
2. I believe I can become good at anything I choose to put my mind to
3. I maintain a positive emotional state of mind regardless of what is going on around me
4. I push through fear to accomplish things that are uncomfortable
5. What I do is aligned to a deeply held sense of purpose
6. I make the most of life by using my time wisely
7. I am like a battery, always full of energy and ready to go
8. I enjoy trusting, respectful relationships with everyone in my life

	STRONGLY DISAGREE	DISAGREE	NEUTRAL	AGREE	STRONGLY AGREE
1	☐	☐	☐	☐	☐
2.	☐	☐	☐	☐	☐
3.	☐	☐	☐	☐	☐
4.	☐	☐	☐	☐	☐
5.	☐	☐	☐	☐	☐
6.	☐	☐	☐	☐	☐
7.	☐	☐	☐	☐	☐
8.	☐	☐	☐	☐	☐

Even though it's good to know your start point, there's no need to judge it. Just imagine if you could nudge your scores further to the right? And just imagine what life would be like if you could live it way over to the right-hand column most of the time. That's our goal together.

Wherever you'd like to develop, there's a book in the Own Life collection for you. By fully participating in this book (*OWN LIFE WITH TRUST*) you'll begin to enjoy more trusting and respectful relationships.

In the future, if you'd like to work on: accepting yourself for who you are or, becoming the person you want to be grab the book titled *OWN LIFE WITH CONFIDENCE*. If you want to manage your emotions and push through fear, then pick up *OWN LIFE WITH COURAGE*. And if you would like to engineer a lifestyle that fulfils your dreams, then *OWN LIFE WITH PURPOSE* is the next book to add to your collection.

Now you have your baseline, are you ready to live a more rewarding life? Sure you are. Let's jump into *OWNING LIFE WITH TRUST.*

CHAPTER 1
YOUR RELATIONSHIP RESERVOIR

Start by taking an audit of the people you share your life with. Do they fill your emotional reservoir, or deplete it? How can you increase the inflow of energy from those people who nourish you? How can you plug the drains of those that sap your enjoyment?

Who Is in Your Life?
You are sailing through life on a cruise ship, and you share it with a whole host of characters. Each room represents a different aspect of your life; some people don't move between rooms, some do. Let's give a name to each room and list the people that you can find there. Examples of room titles are work, family, neighbours, old friends, gym mates, fellow gamers, etc.

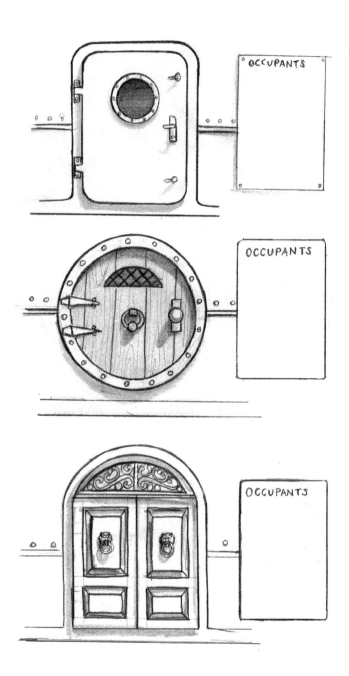

Reflect & Write: Look at the illustration on the previous page and give each door a name, and then list the people who you can meet behind it.

Your life satisfaction right now is largely due to the people you wrote down on your lists. This is who you spend your time with. These are the people who you want to be appreciated by. When you enter a room and spend time there, do you come out uplifted, or drained? Perhaps it depends on who specifically is in the room.

So, who is it that builds you up and makes you feel good? Put a '+' next to their name. Who leaves you feeling worse? Put a '-' next to their name.

How does it feel to 'rate' people? You're judgemental because I'm asking you to be. But let's be clear about what you are rating. The symbol that you have put next to a name isn't a judgement of that person. It is a judgement of the nature of your relationship with them – it is your feelings that you've been rating. How you feel is down to you. Sure, behaviours of others will trigger an emotional reaction, and from time to time you will say 'they make me feel... '

But you can't control them, and they can't control you. You can influence them, and they can influence you. In this book, we'll explore how you can create a separation between the behaviour of someone else and how you feel; and on the flip side, how you can behave so that others would attach a '+' symbol to your name.

Everyone is Unique and Imperfect

By this point in life, you'll have noticed that you're not perfect, and you know you never will be. You've been socially conditioned. You have bad habits that are hard to shake. You have down days and up days. Your emotions get triggered by external events. You have a unique set of values and beliefs. In fact, you're wonderfully, magically unique, and all those lumps and bumps and idiosyncrasies make you YOU. And this is what makes the human race so frustratingly amazing.

And it's not just you. EVERYONE is unique. They may say they're fine, but often this is not true. Everyone is carrying with them some sense that, in some way, they're not OK; and that in some way, they too are struggling. So, let's quieten the voice of judgement. Their behaviour isn't because of you, at its root is something about themselves.

But this is hard because evolution has planted a trick inside us. We all pattern match and make assumptions about people based on our past experiences. A series of experiments by Princeton psychologists Janine Willis and Alexander Todorov[2] reveal that all it takes is a tenth of a second to form an impression of a stranger from their face. Then, because subconsciously we're then looking for evidence that our initial assessment was right – longer exposure doesn't significantly alter those first impressions, they simply boost confidence in the initial judgement.

One of the traits we judge in the blink of an eye is whether we trust the other person or not, and trust is at the foundation of good relationships. Take a look at the four characters, who are you most likely to trust and why?

No one is the same as you, and the greater the differences appear to be the more we feel uncomfortable. When we enter a room of strangers, we are drawn to people we perceive to be similar to ourselves – we have to bring conscious effort to want to get to know the people who are different. You have to bring conscious effort to re-see people, with fresh eyes, to honour and respect their differences and their right to believe, value, and behave differently to you. Sometimes you'll remember to do this, and often you won't.

It's the same for others too. They formed a first impression about you, their subconscious is pattern matching, and it takes time for them to reform an opinion as they get to know the real you.

When you see another person for who they really are, beyond their clothing and projected persona, you'll find the universal truth that everyone, at some point, has struggled with every topic covered in the Own Life Collection: Confidence, Courage, Purpose and Trust. You will find that we are more alike than you have ever realised. As a species, we're a family of human beings with common desires and motives; as individuals, we are full of wonderful idiosyncrasies. Your ability to hold both truths in your mind is the key to believing you can enjoy wonderful relationships with anyone that you meet.

Reflect & Write: Which 10 people do you spend the most time with? Do they boost your emotional energy, or do they drain it? Plot their names beneath the mood line.

Stepping back to take in the whole picture; your emotional state is a reflection of the weight on the line. If you have more weight on the right, you are likely to feel good. More weight on the left, and you are likely to feel drained. The goal, therefore, is to shift the weight to the right. Of course, it would be wonderful to simply spend all of your time with people who quite naturally boost your emotional energy, but things aren't always that straightforward. You need to find ways to both reduce the emotional drain of the relationships that aren't currently working, while also maximising the energy boost that you get from naturally positive relationships.

Never Too Much of a Good Thing

Reflect & Write: Who brings out the best in you? Who makes you feel good? Select five people who boost your emotional energy, and then be precise about what positive emotions they invoke in you. (Do they bring: amusement, delight, elation, excitement, happiness, joy, pleasure, affection, empathy, friendliness, love, courage, hope, humility, satisfaction, trust, calmness, contentment, relaxation, relief, and serenity?)

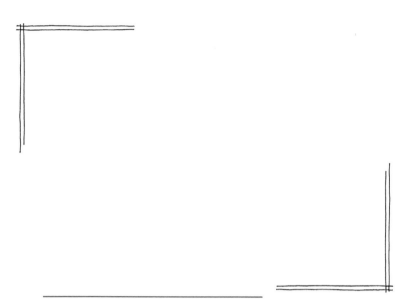

Reflect & Write: The relationship is likely reciprocal – you boost their emotional energy in some way. So, what do you do for them? Think of each person in turn – how do you make them feel good?

These relationships are entirely positive for both of you, and the effect of spending time together boosts your entire system. With these people, you genuinely can't have too much of a good thing. So, let's go for 10 per cent more.

This can either be 10 per cent more time in total or bringing 10 per cent more quality to the time that you do have together. Quality comes from the level of attention that you both bring to one another. I spend a lot of time with my wife, and during the vast majority of that time, our focus is on our children. Drinking a coffee while sitting down one-on-one with no phones, or kids, or to-do lists, just once a day, would increase the quality of our connection by at least 10 per cent.

Reflect & Write: What can you do to increase the quality or quantity of connection that you have with your top five energy boosters?

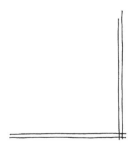

Water the Flowers, Not the Weeds

When you take a watering can to the garden, you deliberately pour the water on the flowers you want to flourish. This is what you're doing in the exercise above: considering which relationships you want to nurture and blossom, and therefore being deliberate about where you place your focus.

Weeds grow in your garden too: they suck nutrients from the ground, stunt the growth of the flowers, and take up space and light. You don't take your watering can and pour water on them. In life, some individuals take your light and suck your nutrients, so why feed them with your attention and emotional energy?

Reflect & Write: Who drains your energy? What weeds are you watering? Bring them into your mind and write down how it feels to be thinking about them now.

Stepping back and looking at what you have written in the box above, has your style of writing changed from the previous exercises? How hard you pressed on the page? The size of the lettering? Exclamation marks? Formation of letters?

You'll probably find the inner emotions come straight through you, down your arm and out of your pen. Your inner state of mind has affected your behaviour – in this instance, it's just how you wrote, and only you can notice the subtle difference. This person you've been thinking about isn't with you now, has done nothing in the last five minutes to trigger the change in your behaviour, and yet your behaviour is altered simply by your memory of them.

Later in the book, we'll look at how you can alter your relationships with 'difficult' people. For now, though, notice which relationships you're watering. Does most of your attention go to those people who build you up? Or do you water the weeds by allowing uncomfortable memories to constantly resurface and affect your state of mind?

If you're like many people, you'll spend a huge amount of time replaying bad situations, spinning them this way and that. Sometimes at night. Sometimes all night! Round and round they go, causing negative moods. Causing you not to see the flowers at all. All your water is falling on the weeds. If you explained it to someone else, you'd fear being judged as petty, and told to 'just get over it'. But you can't. It eats away at you. When this happens to me I find the only solution is to give it my full attention for a short period of time. I take a blank sheet of paper and write down all the thoughts that come into my head, in whatever order they happen to come out. I'm not attempting to get to a solution or to write a coherent report, I'm just letting my words flow as fast as the thoughts emerge.

You'll have a go at this in a minute, the trick isn't to be writer and editor at the same time – your hand is just the transcriber of the voice inside your head.

Reflect & Write: Choose the biggest weed in your life, the one that gets the inner emotions boiling, and simply begin to transcribe what comes up.

You started off fast, right, and then things slowed, and then there was a burst of speed as another thing came up. Then you paused. Then you said 'AND ANOTHER THING...' And eventually, nothing new came up. Everything that has been spinning around your mind is on the page. You can take a step back and say, 'Yes, that's it.'

When you look at the page, you observe the outpouring of your 'chimp mind'. It's fuelled by emotion. I find that when these thoughts have literally come straight out of my head and are looking back at me from the page I can find some emotional separation. It's as though the rational human within me can observe the chimp as separate from myself, and the chimp settles down, knowing it has been fully heard and respected.

Nothing externally is fixed, of course. But you're laying the groundwork for the fixing to begin by acknowledging the emotion, but not being controlled by it. This leads us beautifully into the next section as we'll see that at times throughout our life, our childish emotions take over and control our behaviour and this is true for your 'difficult' people too.

CHAPTER 2
WHEN THERE'S NO RESPECT

Some relationships are lop-sided; one person feeling inferior to another in certain ways, and therefore somehow being dependent on the other.

You can observe this dynamic in all childhood relationships; we all can play the superior or inferior partner, and we can all be triggered into either role throughout our adult life. By using the lens of transactional analysis,[3] we'll deconstruct what's happening and learn how to rebalance things so there is mutual respect.

Transactional Analysis

When you were born, what could you do? Practically nothing! You were completely dependent on grown-ups to give you nourishment and safety and love. At this point in life, you had no language to explain things rationally – you simply had feelings. The grown-ups did something, and you felt an emotion, and it caused you to cry or scream or smile or giggle.

Eric Berne would call this a transaction: one person did something, and a second person had a reaction. His 1964 book *Games People Play*[4] coded these transactions, and we'll be borrowing from his work and terminology to dig a little deeper into what causes a lack of respect in some relationships.

Berne talks about our ability to transact from one of three states throughout our life: the child, the parent and the adult. Furthermore, he explains how each state naturally triggers a corresponding state in the other person.

First, let's explore the child state. As infants, we are small, helpless and dependent. We have internal reactions to external events, and this emotional body of data remains with us for life. We experience grown-ups (in Berne's language – 'Parents'), and they appear superior to us in every way. Their appraisals of us go in unfiltered, we're not equipped to judge them, so we form a picture of ourselves by how others react to us. All of this is unshakeable. Our child is with us every moment for the rest of our lives and can be triggered at any moment. Sometimes the child that gets triggered is our joyful, creative, imaginative, giggling child; and sometimes it is the criticized, judged, belittled, dependent child (like when someone points out that we're not acting like responsible adults).

As we grow up, we record all the behaviours, actions, sayings and habits of the people around us. This forms the basis of the 'Parent State', which can be triggered within us throughout life. If you have siblings you may have received from them the words of your parents even when you were both children. My five-year-old son Wilbur now says to his 11-year old sister, 'Olive, you can't go on your phone until you've done your homework.' He's recorded the authoritative voice of his parents; tone, timing and all! You too can bring out your authoritative voice when it's required – the voice of superiority.

We'll come to the adult state later, but first, we'll explore the dynamics between two people, one of who is in the child state, and one in the parent state. In a moment I'll ask you to recall when you've experienced each state, but first a story to bring it to life.

It's 6:45 am on a Sunday in summer. Five-year-old Olive and I come downstairs to have breakfast. She goes to the fridge and pulls out a full bottle of water.

'What's that?' I ask

'My special water,' responds Olive.

'I can see that, but we don't drink bottled water, we drink water from the tap,'

'But it's my special water, Dad.'

'Look, sweetheart, it's sparkling water, you don't even like sparkling water,' I say, taking the bottle from her.

'No, Dad, it's mine,' says my slightly upset child.

'Look, darling,' I say, bending down to get close to her face, 'it says here SP, that's the start of the word 'Sparkling'. You don't like sparkling water.'

At this point she takes the bottle from my hand and moves to begin to open it, 'Dad, it's my special water.'

'There's water in the tap, here's a glass, now sit down,' I say authoritatively, retaking the bottle and firmly putting it back into the fridge.

Sometime later, with my inner voice still recounting the incident and souring my mood, my wife walks in. Goes to the fridge. Takes out the bottle of water. Hands it to Olive, 'Olive, you didn't tell Dad about your special water!'

In this scenario, I was in the critical superior parent state, causing Olive to be in the criticized inferior child state. I had given her no space or respect. If I had, I would have understood that the previous day, while out shopping, her mum had bought and finished a sparkling bottle of water. Wanting to 'be like Mum', Olive too had wanted to drink from a bottle. So they refilled it – put it in the fridge so it was perfectly cold, and agreed that 'first thing tomorrow morning, let Dad know that your special water is in the fridge'.

Reflect & Write: When (recently) have you been pushed into the small, dependent, criticized child position? When have you been in Olive's shoes? How does it feel?

Reflect & Write: How about when you were in my position, taking the superior parent position? In the moment, it might have felt powerful, but reflecting on it, knowing that you caused the other person to feel like a controlled, inferior child. How does it feel?

Neither are great places to be, right? And it's easy to see how, when one person takes the critical parent position, the other person naturally falls into the criticized child role. Many people complain of micromanagement and this is the reason, they feel they are being treated like a child; under-trusted, under-respected, and undervalued.

It works the other way around too. By taking a dependent child position, the natural response is for the other person to become the parent. Let's take a look at the work scenario.

'Hey, Boss. I'm really struggling with this thing. I just can't do it, and I'm really worried that I'll mess it up.'

'OK. Give it to me, I'll do it, don't worry about it.'

The employee comes to the boss as a helpless, dependent

child, and the boss's natural parental instincts kick in to take the pain away from their 'child'. But what have we now set up? This dynamic gets repeated – the employee doesn't tackle anything challenging, their self-confidence gets lower. The boss takes on more and more work that really should be delegated but can't for fear of stressing the employee. It's an unhealthy working relationship that serves neither party.

That's enough of the theory. Let's look at the relationships in your life through this parent-child lens.

When You Are the Child

Reflecting on the whole spectrum of relationships that you have – peers, colleagues, neighbours, family members, siblings, friends, lecturers, receptionists, boss, subordinates – with whom do you have a parent-child relationship where you are often in the child position? Look for relationships where the balance of power lies with the other person, or you look up to them; or where you are dependent in some way; or where they 'mother you'; or where you are taken 'under someone's wing'.

Some of these may feel nurturing and loving rather than oppressive and critical – but nevertheless, the dynamic isn't of mutual respect, one person is perceived by both of you as superior.

Reflect & Write: 'People who are 'parents' to my 'child' are...

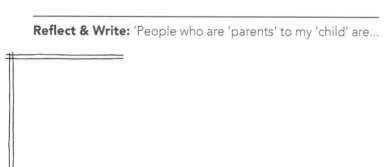

While some relationships are fixed with this dynamic, in other relationships, the situation dictates what role each of you take. When it comes to our social life, my wife is the boss. I am happy to defer all decision-making to her and I go where I'm told we're going. When it comes to where we spend our summer holiday as a family, the roles are reversed.

Considering your most important relationship, can you identify situations where you play the role of the child (willingly or not!).

Reflect & Write: 'Situations when I am the child include...'

When You Are the Parent

Who do you look after? Who needs you to function effectively? Who can't be trusted on their own? With whom do you feel you need to put on your 'bossy' hat?

Reflect & Write: Identify five people from any area of your life and consider why you find yourself in the 'parent' position.

As you parent them more, do you find that they act more childishly? You can get caught in a loop that is serving neither of you, and may allow resentment to simmer.

Habitual Positions

You play different positions at different moments, and with different people. But do you have a strong default position? I know my tendency is towards 'parenting' and I very infrequently find myself in the child role. In the past, my parenting bias has resulted in feedback about a perception of superiority, arrogance or ego. If I am to have positive relationships, it's clearly something that I need to bring conscious attention to.

Reflect & Write: Can you spot strong habitual positions in others? Who in your network is a stereotypical 'parent' (likes to be in charge) or stereotypical 'child' (is dependent on others)?

Reflect & Write: What about you? Do you have a bias towards one or the other? Or perhaps there's a clear link between the situation and your role. Take some notes about your natural tendencies in different situations.

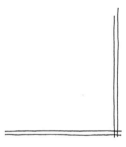

You'll notice how default children (who are dependent on others), would be attracted to a default parent (who likes to be in control), and vice-versa. Many marriages last for many years based on this principle. You may have heard phrases like 'she wears the trousers', or 'he's under the thumb', which describe 'parent'-'child' marriages (and both of which sound very old fashioned and sexist).

The Effect of Hierarchy

You're at school or university with a group of peers about to embark on a team project as equals. Then one of you is nominated as the leader. In an instant, there's a hierarchy. The physiology of the leader instantly changes; the mind says, 'I am responsible' and the natural position to take is that of 'parent'. In the same instant, everyone else is transported to the 'child' state. They sit back in their chair, relax and wait for the leader to take charge.

This is damaging for everyone involved, and if it's allowed to deepen, the team will not function effectively. The leader will become 'the boss', feeling the need to control and micromanage a collection of subordinates who feel belittled and under-valued.

Other circumstances automatically trigger the parent-child dynamic, including interviewer and interviewee; teacher and student; and in many cultures, we can add age, gender, and social class.

Parent-child dynamics are everywhere, and are the default setting in many circumstances, particularly in organizational hierarchies. But they are built on inequality and a lack of mutual respect.

Adult-to-Adult Relationships

Thankfully, relationships don't have to be parent-child. Eric Berne introduced a third position from which we can interact with people. He called this the 'adult state'. You know what an adult-to-adult relationship looks and feels like. In the earlier section Never Too Much of a Good Thing you identified five people who boost your energy, and you boost theirs.

Reflect & Write: When you consider each of those people, what words come to mind that describes the relationship and how it feels?

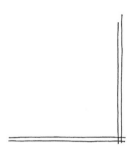

When you are in the adult state, you are aware of the input available from your 'child' and your 'parent' and can bring rational thought to your actions. When the other person is also in the adult state, this feels easy because there is mutual respect and a sense of equality.

Behaving Like an Adult

If you're locked in a parent-child dynamic, how do you shift it to adult-adult? Berne's book is called *Games People Play*, and the goal of the game he refers to is to maintain the current stable (if ineffective) relationship. People have grown up knowing how to play their game, without even knowing they were playing one at all. It is built into the fabric of our culture. How do you break the game? Change the rules. If you don't feed the child, they learn how to feed themselves. If you don't depend on the parent, they lose the ability to control you.

You change the rules by always playing from the adult position, regardless of which position the other person interacts with you from. Because you break the rules, the other person can't continue to be a parent or child. After some resistance (because they've got deeply ingrained habits), their only option is to meet you in the adult space.

If you find yourself in the child space, your emotions are controlling you. If you find your life is run by your out-of-control emotions, check out *OWN LIFE WITH COURAGE* where you'll learn strategies to manage your internal state.

If you find yourself acting like a parent, ask yourself how you can decrease the perceived dependence of the other person. Is the root cause because you have an overcontrolling tendency, or because the other person has a feeling of inferiority? What would happen if you showed greater faith in their potential?

Reflect & Write: You have already identified several relationships where the dynamic is parent-child. What actions can you take to move your position? And how do you imagine the other person would respond?

CHAPTER 3
HANDLING CONFLICT

When you disagree with someone, what happens next? If you're afraid of conflict, perhaps you back down even before they know you have a different point of view. If you're too comfortable with conflict, perhaps you charge straight in and end up in an argument that damages your relationship. In this section you'll learn to notice that different perspectives are inevitable, and become more comfortable in engaging in constructive conflict which values the insights that everyone brings. The following quote from Dudley Field Malone sets the spirit that we'll take with us over the next few pages: 'I have never in my life learned anything from any man who agreed with me.'

My Relationship to Conflict

I hear many people say, 'I don't like conflict'.

Reflect & Write: Do you? When there is conflict or the early signs that a conflict may be brewing, what do you do?

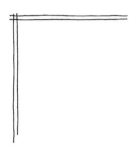

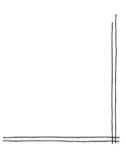

When we're uncomfortable with conflict, we tend to employ one of five strategies:

1. Compromise (a bit of your idea, and a bit of mine)
2. Fake blindness (there is no conflict)
3. Ignore it (just move on)
4. Defer it (get someone else to decide)
5. Fight it out (attempt to win the debate)

Reflect & Write: Consider each of the strategies in turn and attempt to find an example from your past when you have employed each of them.

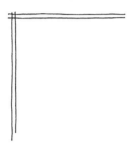

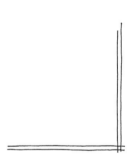

Perhaps you found it easy to come up with examples of some strategies and they might be your 'conflict default state'. The second one on the list is interesting. A large minority will say 'I don't have conflict in my life.' But I don't believe this is actually true. We first have to define what conflict is, and then we'll notice that it's everywhere in our lives.

'Conflict' includes two armies fighting across a border; political parties fighting an election; Pepsi vs Coke; creationism vs evolution; and many more. In most of these cases, there is evidence of conflict because of 'clear-to-see' actions.

Have you ever had conflicting thoughts with yourself? 'I should go to the gym; not today though.' To other people, there is no obvious sign of this conflict – it's one of internal thought.

Have you ever negotiated with someone else about where you will go for dinner? Or what to watch on Netflix? When we consider the word 'conflict', our definition is: 'two or more people have different thoughts about something'.

With this refined definition of the word 'conflict', can you accept that it's everywhere, every day and that at times you are blind to it? Even the people you love the most will have different perspectives to you.

Reflect & Write: Considering a very good friend, or your partner, someone whom you respect – what subjects do you have different opinions about?

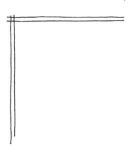

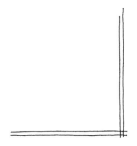

With these people, you simply accept that you have different points of view, without feeling forced to accept their point of view as being correct, (although secretly you'd love them to one day say, 'you were right all along'!).

What if they don't really listen to your point of view? What if, when you are making your case they're clearly not listening, instead they are just waiting for you to pause for breath so they can restate their case? What if you never get the space to make your point at all? It may not happen with your trusted friend, but it happens with some people in your network.

Reflect & Write: How does it feel not to be listened to?

Some people seem naturally able to stand tall in conflict, happily articulating their perspective in-depth, and revelling in it (they step into it). Others always shy away from it, go quiet, and disengage from the conversation (they step back from it).

Reflect & Write: Who do you know that sits at either end of this spectrum, and where do you sit?

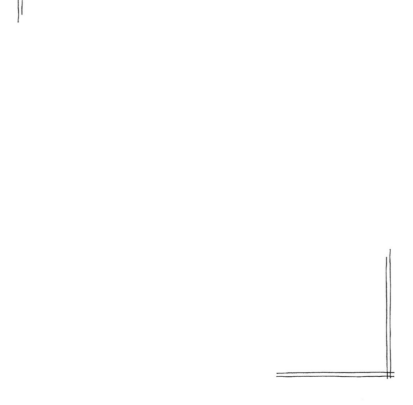

Seeing the Whole

I say 'up', you say 'down'. I say 'black' you say 'white'. I say 'left' you say 'right'. 'Girl'. 'Boy'. 'In'. 'Out'. 'Day'. 'Night'.

When something exists, so does its opposite, and in many instances, a whole range of options between the two. Whatever point of view you hold, a contrary one exists. To understand anything fully we have to acknowledge and then appreciate the other perspectives. Yet to us, sometimes one perspective is so clear that we instantly discount the others. We become blinkered and dismissive, sometimes becoming even more entrenched in our way of seeing if our perspective is challenged. Look at this picture, what do you see?

It's not a trick question. You see a square, with two dotted sides, and two solid sides. If we now imagine that this is 3D, we see a box with two dotted sides and two solid sides. How about in the picture opposite? What does the pirate see?

'I see a dotted box, arghh,' says the Pirate.

'Really, Mr Pirate, the box is clearly solid,' responds Lady Prim of Hampton Court.

'Well, shiver me timbers, Lady Prim, I believe that this time you are not correct. The box is quite clearly dotted.'

'My goodness, Mr Pirate, perhaps the time has arrived for that good eye of yours to be checked. The box is most certainly solid.'

'Oh no, it ain't. It's dashed, and my parrot 'ere agrees with me.'

'It's solid. Now come along, stop being silly, I have things to do.'

'IT AIN'T SOLID, AND I AIN'T GOING NOWHERE WITH THE LIKES OF YOU!'

'Well, there's no need to shout; there is nothing wrong with my hearing, just as there is nothing wrong with my eyes. And if you refuse to come with me, then I shall go alone. Goodbye, Mr Pirate.'

'GOOD RIDDANCE TO YOU, LADY PRIM.'

The origin of all conflict; two people seeing the same thing differently.

In this case, the Pirate wants to fight it out, while Lady Prim is OK to walk away, leaving the conflict unresolved. In this case, as in most cases, the argument ends with each person even more convinced they are right, and even less willing to listen to alternative suggestions.

At the start, Lady Prim and Mr Pirate probably didn't care much about this box – and at the end, they still don't care about it, but are consumed with negative thoughts about the other person. If the objective of the conversation was to establish the true composition of the box, it has been well and truly lost because of their lack of ability to enter the conflict positively; from the adult space.

Have you ever found yourself defending a position that you didn't know you had before a conversation began? In fact, have you ever found yourself passionately arguing for a point of view that you actually don't believe in, just because you don't want to back down?! Sure you have!

Back to our box. If our pirate beckoned all his shipmates forward to stand right alongside him, what do they see? A dotted box! Have these other perspectives helped us to establish the composition of the box? No. Yet they would be in wonderful agreement because they see things the same way.

What if Lady Prim was off taking afternoon tea with Lord Prim, and couldn't offer her different perspective? All 20 pirates see a dotted box, and therefore it must be dotted.

You see the danger of working with teams who all see things the same way.

To see the whole picture, we must seek to work with people who have different perspectives – in corporate-speak, this is termed 'diversity'. The word is often combined with the word 'inclusion', which means enabling all the voices to be heard.

Even the quiet ones. Especially the quiet ones! When we have diversity, and we have inclusion, then conflict is inevitable – different perspectives will be brought into the open, and the team will get a full picture of a situation. In a group situation, if there is diversity, and there is no conflict, what is going on?

It's because there is a parent-child dynamic. Some people feel inferior, belittled, undervalued, disrespected and therefore don't speak up. They are in the child position. If this is the case in your group – how do you maintain an adult space and enable others to move from parent to adult so that all the voices can be heard?

Giving People a Voice
Reflect on a group of people you spend time with. This could be your team at work, or a project group at Uni, or even a group of mates. It's likely that within the group, some people speak their mind readily – and you know their point of view on most things that come up. What about the quietest person in the group? They may outwardly appear to agree with the rest of the group, but they haven't shaped the direction of the conversation. When there is lots of boisterous chatter, it's easy for individual voices to be lost. The group loses a valuable perspective and the individual feels worthless.

Reflect & Write: Who is in this position, and what can you do to help them have their voice heard? If it is you who is silent, what can you do to bring your perspectives to the table?

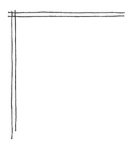

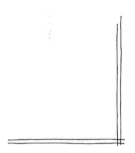

We All See the World Differently

In the example above it's clear that the pirate and Lady Prim see things differently because they're standing in different positions, and therefore the visual sensory information received is different. However, even if the pirate and Lady Prim stood side by side, their five senses receiving the same inputs, they would have different internal representations of what they see. How does this work?

In our brains, the reticular activating system (RAS) connects the brain stem to the cerebral cortex through various neural paths. If our consciousness were flooded with all the sensory information available to it then it would be overwhelmed and unable to make any decisions. So the RAS filters and prioritizes information coming from the external world, controlling what appears in the mind's eye at any point of time. These filters depend on your life experiences, and therefore, everyone has a unique set. This is why people have a different internal representation of what they experience in the outside world.

The sensory information being received by the guy in the top picture and the woman in the lower one is the same, yet their RAS filters are different. What they see in their mind's eye isn't a true representation of what's in front of them. The mind is working more like a projector than a camera. What the guy sees is a friendly social situation with lots of interesting people to meet. The woman sees a threatening situation with lots of opportunities to feel uncomfortable.

How you see things is guaranteed to be different from

how someone else sees them. Sometimes these differences are obvious; sometimes subtler. We can't possibly see what another person sees, yet we assume we can because we're looking at the same thing. The only possible way to understand a different perspective is to ask the question: how do you see things? And then to listen with a truly open mind.

Jumping to Conclusions

Stephen Covey said, 'We judge ourselves by our intentions and others by their behaviour.' But what else can we use to judge someone on? We can only judge what we see; we're not mind-readers. But for ourselves, even if the specific action we take came out a little different than we'd hoped it would, we can console ourselves that at least our intentions were good.

The observable action comes as a consequence of thought processes that we often cut short. From time to time, we jump to conclusions. Some people do this often, others less frequently. But we all do it.

Reflect & Write: Think of the last time you jumped to a conclusion about something that later turned out to be wrong.

Organizational psychologist Chris Argyris developed a model called the 'Ladder of Inference'[5] (first published by Peter Senge[6]) which helps to explain and then correct what's going on.

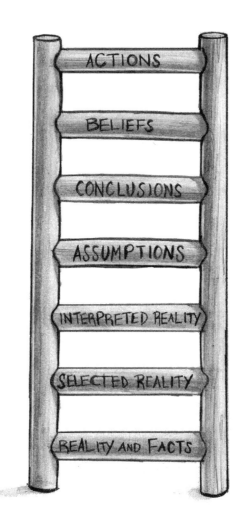

Starting at the bottom of the ladder, we receive sensory inputs through our five senses, which pass through the RAS filters to give us a selective reality. We add meaning in order to interpret reality through our cultural lens and apply our existing assumptions. Based on these, we draw conclusions, from which we form beliefs, and take actions that seem 'right' because they are aligned with our beliefs.

Wow, you see how far it is from facts to actions! When someone behaves in a certain way and you can't understand why, it's because the nature of the rungs on your ladder are different to theirs. The sequence is the same, but the outputs are different.

When you jump to a conclusion, it's because the rungs are working super-fast in your sub-conscious. The key to success is to slow down and allow your conscious mind to ask questions at each step. This is also the key to understanding someone else's behaviour. Remember, they believe that they are doing the right thing because it is aligned with their beliefs – so challenging them at this level can be perceived to be an attack on their belief system, causing a dramatic and disproportionate response.

You may have used the phrase 'they're making a mountain out of a molehill' because you think you are talking about a minor action, but they interpret it as an attack on their beliefs. If your conclusions are different to someone else's, carefully descend the ladder with them until you can get back to reality and the facts that you can both agree on, and then climb the ladder together comparing notes about what you both now see as you climb.

Reflect & Write: Think of three situations where someone acted in a certain way, and you couldn't understand the logic of their behaviour. Who was it? What was the situation? What did they do? And how can you climb the ladder with them so that you can understand the belief on which it is based?

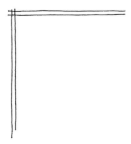

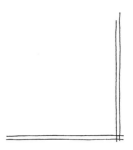

Good Conflict

It's only when two people use the 'fight it out' strategy that a difference of opinions becomes a heated argument. The opposing points of the two sides are out in the open, but nobody is listening and learning. With all the other strategies that are employed to avoid conflict at least one of the points of view goes unheard. So, what is the right strategy?

Step 1 – Seek to Understand

Henry Ford shares the thought: 'If there's any one secret to success, it lies in the ability to get the other person's point of view.' When we say, 'get it', we mean really get it. This means noticing how our ladder of inference is working as they are talking. What assumptions are we making? What filters are working to distort the reality of their words? We don't want our interpretation of their reality, what Ford is talking about is the ability to stand in their shoes to experience their reality.

Here's an important point. By listening and enquiring you do not necessarily agree with their point of view, you are simply expanding your awareness of the viewpoints that can be held.

Aristotle said, 'An educated mind can entertain a thought without accepting it.' The language you use with the other person makes it clear that you are exploring their reality by using the word 'you' or 'yours' a lot. 'How do you see things?' 'What conclusions are you drawing?' 'What assumptions underpin your conclusions?' 'What facts support your thinking?'.

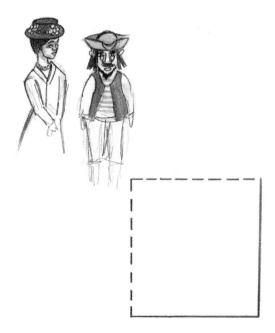

The test is that you can explain their argument back to them with detail and clarity that is surprising. Allow them to make tweaks to your words until they are completely satisfied that they have been fully heard and understood.

In the first step, you make the other person feel great – they are being respected, honoured and valued. But there are some typical traps that can catch you out even at this stage:

Defensiveness: Can you really listen when you feel as though you need to defend yourself from an attack?

Inner Voice: Your inner voice will be chattering away, and therefore preventing you from giving them your full attention.

Time: Your internal clock will be ticking. If you only have 10 minutes for this topic, and you spend all of it exploring the other person's argument, then where does that leave you?

Therefore you leap ahead, make assumptions, and jump to conclusions.

You will notice that you are in control of all the things that could derail this first step.

Step 2 – Invite an Invitation to Share

Make it clear that you have another perspective (notice the non-confrontational choice of words: it's simply a different way of seeing things), and then ensure you fully do step 1. Keep asking the questions, keep being inquisitive until you really can explain the other position better than they can. When the conversation starts, you could use words like: 'We see things differently. I would love to explore your perspective so I can really get where you're coming from, and only then, give you some space to ask me a bunch of questions that help me to articulate my thoughts to you. If this means that we need to find some more time to continue the conversation, would you be open to that?'

The groundwork is laid. There is a subtle moral contract in place: I will listen to you, and then you will listen to me.

The only thing that derails this step is if you skip it or do it too late. You need to set the agenda so it's clear for both of you. If you don't then a) the other person may not know you have an alternative point of view to share, and b) they will think that spending so much time on their opinion means it's the only one that matters.

Step 3 – Share the Full Ladder

Help the other person to see what you see. Remember that they have different filters, so their RAS produces a different 'selected reality' to yours. Talk through your assumptions, allow your interpreted reality to be tested. The goal isn't to get them to change their mind but to help them to see what it is that you see so that they can explain it back to you.

What will derail you here is that the other person probably hasn't read this book. They will be flipping from parent to child – interrupting, not listening, and generally hijacking the agenda to reiterate their view of the world. It's an ingrained habit, so give them a break and continue to hold the adult space: 'Thanks for the interruption, and for reiterating the importance of this specific point to you / for adding a new thought. Let me check I still fully understand your point of view, and then let's return to you helping me to articulate my thoughts to you.'

Be patient. It may take a few rounds of holding the adult space for them to realize that the old games that have worked for years are no longer being played.

At this point most conflicts melt away. The misunderstanding, the misinterpretation, the misalignment, the lack of respect that causes the vast majority of conflict (or the avoidance of conflict), is gone. In the tiny minority of cases, a decision needs to be taken and it's a clear choice between going one way or another. The conflict ends when a decision is taken, based on all the available facts, a full awareness of all the different perspectives. It may go your way, it may not, but you and everyone else will feel as though their contribution was valued.

Summary

When there is more than one person, there is more than one perspective on anything and everything. If the perspectives are not aired, you're missing an essential ingredient that has helped homo sapiens to evolve. Having the ability to embrace conflicting points of view, to explore them with an open mind and an open heart is a wonderful skill to aspire to and develop. Perhaps you don't have a great relationship with conflict – yet.

Reflect & Write: What will it take for you to develop a more adult relationship with the concept of conflict? To embrace the value of conflict, what will you begin to do?

CHAPTER 4
DEALING WITH UNACCEPTABLE BEHAVIOUR

At some time in your life you've said 'I can't believe they just did that', and you've thought it on many occasions. What did you do about it? What should you do about it? What will you do about it?

Reflect & Write: When have you witnessed, or been on the receiving end of unacceptable behaviour? What is unacceptable behaviour to you?

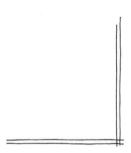

Do those people accept that their behaviour is unacceptable? What are the possible answers to this question?

1. They do it with full awareness that their behaviour is unacceptable and yet are unrepentant.
2. They know they are acting inappropriately and feel guilty inside.
3. They are aware of their actions but do not categorize it as 'unacceptable'.
4. They lack self-awareness that their actions are considered by others to be 'unacceptable'.

Reflect & Write: Test the above assumptions to see if they do cover all your experiences of unacceptable behaviour. Consider four specific instances when someone has acted unacceptably. Who was it? What did they do? Which of the categories does it fall into (1–4)?

When these things happen, you have two options:

1. Rise above it, let it go and manage your own internal state so that you're not negatively affected by it (Use the strategies in *OWN LIFE WITH COURAGE*).
2. Give feedback.

Principles of Feedback

It may be natural to judge the person, categorising them as 'bad', but it's important to separate the person from the action. It's a person's behaviour, rather than their personality, that should be the subject of the feedback. Principle number one, therefore, is to be very specific about the behaviour that you feel is unacceptable.

Who is doing the judging? That's you! Not society, or 'everyone', or 'a few of us'. You must take ownership of your judgement rather than hiding it. And remember that your judgement comes through your life filters – your subjective reality, your assumptions, and your beliefs about what is right and what is wrong. The feedback is more about you than it is about 'them'.

Nobody can control you, and you can't control another person. You can give the gift of feedback in a perfectly empathetic way, but whether it is well received or not cannot be your responsibility. They can choose to change, or they can choose not to. That's their prerogative.

A Model for Feedback

There are several different models for giving feedback, most with acronyms that spell something memorable – and all of them pretty much saying the same thing.

Observation: Explain, with simple clarity, the specific action you have observed.

Feeling: Describe how you personally felt as a result of this action.

The Ask: Suggest different actions that could be taken next time and be open to exploring options.

You can see how this model removes any judgement about the other person and instead helps them to understand the impact on you. This method works for any of the four categories of unacceptable behaviour because it is conducted from the 'adult' space, and therefore shouldn't trigger the parent or child in the other person.

Reflect & Write: Return to your list of people who have behaved unacceptably. Using the feedback model, consider how you could (in theory) structure your feedback to them.

Practising Feedback

Now you know the theory let's set some homework so that you begin to build the muscle. With everything we introduce in the Own Life books it's better to start small and develop your technique before unleashing it in full. So letting go of any thoughts of anybody that would require deep reserves of courage to address, consider a couple of people with whom you have a good foundation of trust.

Reflect & Write: What specific behaviour would you like to address that would help to deepen your relationship with them?

Twice as Nice

In the last exercise I asked you to think of people who you already had a trusting relationship with, so I bet these people do at least twice as many things that make you feel good as make you feel bad. The feedback model works for these too. Not only does giving positive feedback make the other person feel good, but it is also likely to stimulate them to keep repeating the behaviour more often, and therefore you get to feel great more of the time.

'Thanks for all your help,' is nice to hear. But, by running your feedback through the feedback model first, the impact is doubled. 'Last week, when you saw me getting stressed about everything on my to-do list, you offered me help and took a specific task off my list. I felt a real sense of relief and could sleep better again. If you see me struggle again, I will welcome you asking if I've got too much on my plate.'

Often people simply don't know the positive impact they have on you. So begin to tell them, and watch the smiles grow.

Reflect & Write: Name two people that you'd like to give positive feedback to, and plan what you want to say using the feedback model.

CHAPTER 5
TRUST

When you are in a trusting relationship, oxytocin hormones flow around your brain and you feel safe enough to take risks and expose your vulnerabilities. When there is mistrust your amygdala triggers the fight-or-flight response, adrenaline and cortisol are released, and you feel afraid or angry. The level of trust that exists defines the quality of your relationships, so what is it, how does it develop, and how do you recover it when it is gone?

Let's first get your thoughts out on paper with a series of reflect and write questions.

Reflect & Write: What causes you to trust people? Consider people from both your personal and professional life.

Reflect & Write: When you think of a person you trust wholeheartedly, how does it feel, and as a result, how do you behave around them?

Reflect & Write: How readily do you place your trust in people? Are you over-trusting, trusting all the people all the time and regularly feeling let down? Or, are you tight-fisted with it saying, 'They have to earn my trust'? Place an 'x' on the axis:

OVER-TRUSTING   MISTRUSTING

Reflect & Write: How do you feel about where you have positioned yourself on the axis?

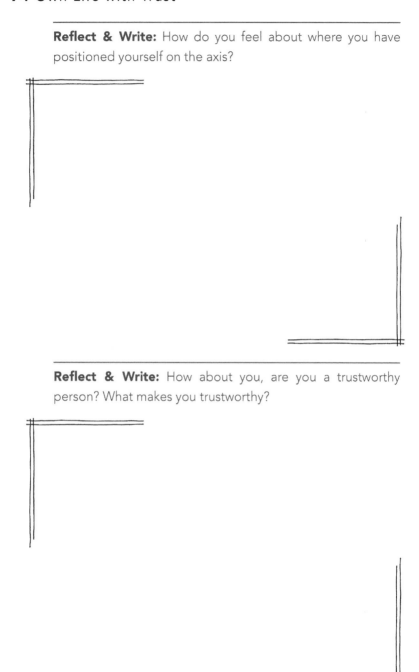

Reflect & Write: How about you, are you a trustworthy person? What makes you trustworthy?

Reflect & Write: Who don't you trust, and specifically, why don't you? Think of three people you don't trust, why not?

Reflect & Write: Notice how it feels to think about how these people betray your trust. How you behave around them is affected by your feelings – when there is mistrust, how do you act?

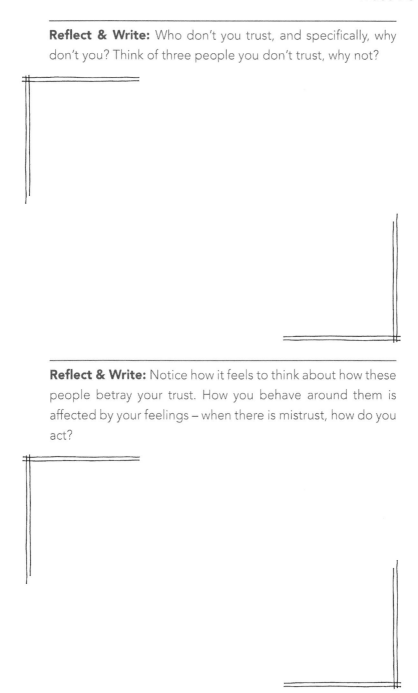

Your Betrayal

Just now you wrote down the reasons why you are trustworthy. However, research by Charles Feltman[7] found that 'we generally judge others to be less trustworthy than ourselves', which means that 'it is very likely that some of the people in your life judge you to be less trustworthy than you consider yourself to be'.

Reflect & Write: How may others consider you to be less than wholly trustworthy? What do you sometimes do to betray the trust that others have in you?

Big gulp! That was slightly sickening to write down. We all want to consider ourselves to be trustworthy, yet some of our actions get in the way. The boot is on the other foot, it's not just other people that betray my trust, I also betray theirs. You are not perfect, and neither are they.

Trust Deconstructed

What is 'trust'? You wrote down a long list of what causes you to trust people, and we use the word 'trust' to summarize the whole list. We then judge a person's character as trustworthy or not. But the basket of attributes that build up the picture of trust is just too jumbled to make sense of. In his wonderfully simple book, *The Thin Book of Trust*,[8] Charles Feltman deconstructs the word 'trust' into four distinct categories. Summarized, they are:

1. Sincere: you are honest; you say what you mean and mean what you say.
2. Reliable: you meet your commitments and keep your promises.
3. Competent: you have the necessary ability to do things well.
4. Caring: you are considerate towards others.

We can now notice how difficult it can be to score full marks across all four 'distinctions'. Let's take the last one, it may be the most important on the list for you and is perhaps the most important one of all. Because you want to really care for other people, do you:

1. Find it difficult to say 'no', and therefore overload yourself and fail to meet some of your commitments?

2. Really try to please people by accepting to do things that you don't have the expertise to do well?
3. Shy away from being honest about how you feel for fear of hurting their feelings?

It may be easy for you to be 100 per cent trustworthy in how you care for people, but at what cost? If you're praising something small ('great, you found the lamp shade') while there's an elephant in the room that you are not addressing, then how much trust is there really?

You may be considered untrustworthy because of a perception of a lack of sincerity, reliability, or competence. It might feel harsh and unfair, but it's exactly how you judge others. The word 'trust' is just too broad to be helpful when we're scrutinising the nature of our relationships – so we're going to use the Feltman distinctions to help move things forward.

You 'Deconstructed'

Earlier you wrote a list of the things that made you trustworthy, and then a second list of the things that made you untrustworthy. These lists may help you with the following assessment.

Reflect & Write: Taking Feltman's four distinctions, write them in order from your strongest to your weakest. Mine would be reliable, competent, sincere, caring. What's your order?

Reflect & Write: What comes last on your list, and how does this affect people's ability to trust you?

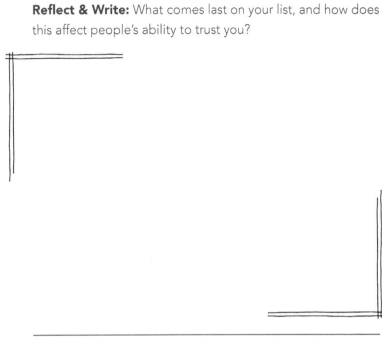

Reflect & Write: Because we have a growth mindset, we can say 'I am not great at this thing... yet.' It will take practice and perseverance to get better, so how will you start?

People Deconstructed

You have relative strengths and weaknesses across the four distinctions, and so do others. Instead of labelling other people as untrustworthy, let's examine what you have observed (not what you have imagined) about others and therefore have a go at ranking their relative strengths and weaknesses.

Reflect & Write: Consider five people who you don't entirely trust. Arrange the list of distinctions from their strongest to their weakest for each person.

Is there a pattern forming? Does the same distinction keep appearing near the end of the list? If so, then you may have an unusually high degree of sensitivity towards betrayal in one dimension. Are you fair, or is your bar of expectation set unreasonably high? Perhaps or perhaps not. By getting into the details, do your feelings towards these people change?

Because I don't always show great compassion for others, I could be labelled as untrustworthy by you, and this label would affect how you behaved around me. With a greater level of insight, you may now say, 'I can completely trust Todd to deliver what he said he would, and with great quality too, however, he sometimes steamrollers in and doesn't listen to other people. I don't feel as though he values or cares about what I have to say.'

Todd is no longer a wholly bad guy (phew!), but he does have some traits that are difficult to accept. Which takes us back around the loop, back to how to deal with unacceptable behaviours. What is your next move? Live with it, or address it with feedback?

The Trust Quality Standard

The International Organization for Standardization develops a set of globally understood and agreed-upon methods for assessing quality. They don't, however, produce international standards for anything like 'how to measure trust'. Which means that every individual is free to set their own standards, and then measure others based on their own definition of quality.

Which is a problem! Because my standards are different from yours. And I sometimes allow myself to bend my own rules:

'I will always ensure the meetings I run end on time as a sign of respect for the commitments that people have following the session... except if it feels like we're ending on a negative tone, then it's OK to carry on.'

'I will be honest and speak my mind... except if I'm afraid of some negative consequences.'

Not only do you not know my standards, but you can also make poor assumptions about my standards based on evidence of my behaviour. But at least there are some generally accepted standards for essential things like timekeeping. Right?

Richard Lewis blogs about how different cultures understand time:

'Time is money, and therefore we shouldn't waste a drop of it', says the New Yorker. 'The sun rises and sets, the moon waxes and wanes, we are born, and we die, and we return in another form – time is endless', says the Tibetan. While the 'Spaniards, Italians and Arabs will ignore the passing of time if it means that conversations will be left unfinished.'[9]

Your cultural upbringing establishes your inner relationship with time. Even with something so measurable and standardized, there is no universal agreement on what constitutes 'good timekeeping'. So there is also no black and white around it – 'lateness' turns out to be subjective based on internal beliefs rather than the position of the hands on a clockface.

Based on your experiences, you've developed a set of assumptions that underpin good and bad behaviour. You then measure others based on your imagination of the 'perfect human', and when someone doesn't measure up to your model of perfection. Boom! They've let you down and are untrustworthy!

Let's backtrack and use the ladder of inference to help us. We're making assumptions – based on what? Our interpreted reality – the one that we have imagined. So, we step down a couple of rungs. What facts or evidence can I use when making an assumption about a person? In the beginning, when you first meet someone, you have very little evidence, so your assumptions should be broad and easily changed. As you begin to get to know someone more, the assumptions can be refined and updated. When they do something you had assumed they wouldn't, then instead of being outraged or surprised, you can simply use the new evidence to update your set of assumptions about them. Nobody is letting you down; they're simply revealing an aspect of themselves that had previously been hidden from you.[10]

Deepening Trust

If there is no mistrust in a relationship then we have the opportunity to consciously grow the level of trust that exists. With some individuals you feel an instant rapport, share surprisingly openly and feel a deep connection with them in almost no time. With other acquaintances, you've maintained a professional separation – you don't really know them, and they don't really know you.

We'll borrow a model first developed by psychologists Joseph Luft and Harrington Ingham in 1955. This model is endearingly known as 'Johari Windows' by combining their first names.[11]

When we're being completely authentic, allowing others to see the true us, then we're operating in an open box – and there may be only a handful of people with whom we

wear no mask. In the majority of our relationships, where trust isn't 100 per cent, we keep things private – work colleagues, flatmates, study partners only get to see the version of us that we want them to see.

Reflect & Write: What are you choosing to hide? And from whom? Make a list.

The level of trust between two people is equal to the combined size of their 'open' boxes. To deepen trust, you slowly and gently begin to reveal parts of yourself, and gently and patiently give the other person the space to share what they feel comfortable to share.

It should be a reciprocal thing and should be allowed to move at a natural pace, but do notice if it has begun to stall or stagnate. If there is no longer any new revealing going on, then you can expect the level of trust between you to flatline – and this may be OK for some relationships.

When you share something with someone that reveals something new about you, then you open the door for them to do the same. Not necessary in the next sentence, or even during the same conversation, but sometime in the future. There's no need to force it, nor suggest that you should do all the revealing while they keep you at arm's length. Trust is a dance that needs both partners to be dancing to the same rhythm, but sometimes someone has to take the lead.

Asking about someone else is, of course, a great way to take the lead. It's often avoided because of a fear of prying (definition: 'inquiring too closely into a person's private affairs'). You will have things that you don't want other people to ask you about, and everyone has these things – so yes, don't pry. When we 'pry a door open', we use a sharp tool and brute strength to force our way through it, however, when you enquire about a person there are loads and loads of doors that are simply waiting to be opened and need zero force. In fact, a great many of them are like automatic doors: you simply walk close to them, and they throw themselves wide open. So yes, don't get the tools out and pry, but don't shy away from all the doors.

Non-prying, inquisitive questions that encourage people to reveal more about themselves in a comfortable disclosure kind of way include:

- Where did you grow up, do you have any brothers or sisters, and what are they like?
- What's the origin of your surname, first name, middle name?

You can take the lead by asking these types of questions in a first meeting, and if you don't know the answer already, you can ask them of people you already know. You can also take the lead by choosing to share something about yourself that is currently hidden. It's hard to plan these things in detail, because then you'll be rehearsing what you want to say, and that will prevent you from coming across as natural and authentic. So instead of deciding what, let's just decide who.

Reflect & Write: Who would you like to expand your 'open' box with when the situation naturally arises?

What To Do When You've Broken Trust

From time to time you break the trust that someone has in you, and it's usually completely unintentional. But remember, you are being judged by your actions and not by your intentions. Furthermore, your actions are being judged against a set of standards that you can't be exactly sure about. It can feel profoundly unfair. Nevertheless, you're aware that someone has lost trust in you, and that hurts. So what should you do about it?

According to Feltman, 'the only known antidote for the betrayal of someone's trust is to acknowledge it and apologize for it.'

Remember you have not suddenly become a wholly untrustworthy person, so find out precisely which of the four 'distinctions' you are perceived (their perception is their reality) to have violated. Then what specifically did you do (or not do)? You are not apologising for being you but how your behaviour has impacted their ability to trust (and therefore feel safe) around you.

Limit the excuse-making; but if the situation has the potential to occur again, be open about it and jointly work through what a better course of action would be. For example: 'Last week I gave you a report that missed some key figures and caused you to be unable to answer key questions from the director. I'm really sorry for not delivering a full report to you, and for causing you some reputational damage in front of other people. I'm also concerned that it may happen again – I rely on getting data from the UK office and haven't found an effective way to influence them. What could I do so that you aren't in the same situation again?'

It may be time for you to eat some humble pie.

Reflect & Write: Who doesn't fully trust you, what has caused that loss of trust, and how can you now rectify it?

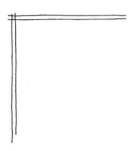

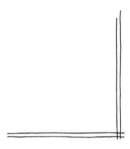

Trust can develop over time, and you can enhance the speed of it by consciously enhancing behaviours across all four distinctions – both in yourself, and using feedback, in others. Remember that your behaviours are driven by your beliefs, but they are being judged through the filters of someone else's life experience. Remove the intense emotion caused by language like 'betrayal of trust', and instead seek to tweak specific behaviours. Be respectful of others' rights to see the world differently.

CHAPTER 6
HOW TO BE INTERESTING

Some people seem adept at entering new groups, striking up a conversation, and connecting well with people. This may not be you, and you'd be in the majority. Say the word 'networking' and the shivers of apprehension start. The art of conversation is an essential life skill yet not one we're taught at school. With a few simple techniques, anyone can be interesting; here we'll learn how.

Reflect & Write: Who do you know that is a good conversationalist, and why do they deserve this accolade?

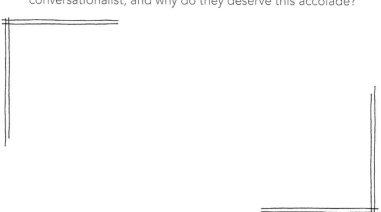

Reflect & Write: What about you? It may be situation-dependent, so reflecting on your recent experiences, when were you a good conversationalist, and when were you not? What made the difference?

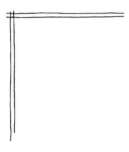

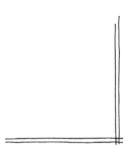

It's pleasing to remember the times when you were a good conversationalist. You probably felt relaxed in the company of the other people and there was mutual respect and a balanced reciprocal nature to listening and talking. When it goes badly, it can feel excruciating, unequal, one-sided, and leaves you feeling under-appreciated or concerned that you came across as a bore.

Reflect & Write: Now, consider the people in your life that are poor conversationalists. What traits do they have in common?

There are a couple of traits that come out most often:

1. They talk too much and don't listen.
2. They are detached and seem disinterested.

To be interesting, simply practise doing the opposite all the time: listen with genuine attention.

Entering New Groups
Think of the last time that you entered a new group. This could be a class at school or college, a new place of work, a team meeting with new colleagues, dinner with the girlfriend's parents or an assessment centre. How did you feel just before entering the room, and what was causing that feeling?

It is the same for almost everyone because we all have the same desire for acceptance. It's hardwired into the animal instincts of all primates because if we're rejected by our clan when we're very young, we die. Our behaviours are driven by a fear of rejection, and so as far as possible, we try to conform so that we 'fit in'.

In a new group, there is no foundation for trust, so individuals are reluctant to be vulnerable. They keep the idiosyncrasies that make them genuinely individual under wraps, and instead engage in 'small talk' about super-safe topics like the weather, rather than the juicy and potentially controversial topic like global warming.

If you feel anxious when joining a group, feel OK about this – it's normal. It's our animal brain keeping us safe from rejection. What happens next is the key. For some people, animal fear overrides natural human instincts to be social, and they create an impenetrable protective bubble around them. The bubble takes different forms – when nervous, some people talk and talk, while others are totally consumed by the internal chatter and are therefore outwardly silent.

If you are consumed by internal negative thoughts which affect your ability to relax in a group, you may want to work through *OWN LIFE WITH COURAGE*. It will help you understand how to overcome your fears and manage your emotional state, as well as learning how to enjoy more positive emotions more often.

Smile – First Impressions Count

Your body language is talking loudly whether you are speaking or not – giving off signals of being welcoming and warm, or cold and hostile. Remember that trust is the foundation stone of any relationship and how you enter a room gives signals of how caring and sincere you are. In this regard, nothing works as powerfully as a simple smile aimed in the direction of each and every person present. They feel acknowledged by you, you begin to make one-on-one connections with the fleeting eye contact that comes with it, and something else happens too – the smiles spread!

So even if your heart is pounding, and the inner voice is chattering – find a way to give a nod and a smile.

Nothing to Say

I once heard a story about an experiment conducted many years ago to test a theory that the most interesting people were those that were interested in others. The organizers of a networking event invited 30 people to an evening of drinks and canapés and afterwards asked the participants to write down the names of three people they found most interesting and would like to be connected with for a follow-up conversation.

Five of the individuals were instructed beforehand to reveal nothing about themselves, to anyone, all evening. If asked something, they deflected the question by asking one of their own back to the other person. When the surveys were collated, and the requests tallied up – who do you think were judged to be the most interesting people in the room?

The five people who had said nothing about themselves!

Carnegie[12] concludes: 'You can make more friends in two months by becoming interested in other people than you can in two years by trying to get other people interested in you'. He continues,[13] 'nothing is as flattering to another person as getting your exclusive attention', and this is brought to life by a third Carnegie quote:[14] 'Mum, I know that you love me very much because whenever I want to talk to you, you stop whatever you are doing and listen to me.'

Is Everyone Interesting?

If you assume that only some people are interesting then you're unlikely to truly follow through with the advice from the last section. Will you turn the conversation over to another person and simply ask questions if you believe that they are boring? No!

What I've found is this. When people don't feel safe they stick to small talk, and this gets very boring very quickly. However, when great trust exists and they feel free to allow their inner thoughts to come tumbling out without fear of judgement – wow, EVERYONE has a story to tell, opinions to share, and passions to get excited about.

When you start with the assumption that everyone is interesting, you can allow your natural curiosity to get to work. If the other person isn't interesting, it's because you haven't laid the foundation for the trust that is necessary for them to open up to you. So enter the dance of trust, be vulnerable yourself, and as you share some of your stories, they'll feel more open to sharing some of theirs.

Reflect & Write: Who have you written off as 'boring'? Can you allow yourself to believe that there is an interesting side to them that you haven't seen yet?

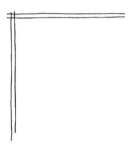

From Small Talk to Deep Stuff

Where are you from? Did you have a long journey? Have you worked here long? What course are you studying? What do you do? Start with any of these questions, get a one-line answer, then a return question: 'How about you?', give a one-line answer. Dialogue over. Uncomfortable silence. Next question from the list. Sound familiar?

To get things really flowing, the secret is to ask a second more inquisitive question before you take your turn to respond to the first one. The second question digs a little deeper, and you get some insight into the real person. You have met plenty of accountants, but behind the job title every one of them is unique, so go looking for the person behind the mask.

Instead of having a bank of one-line questions, develop a set of questions that flow nicely from one to another. Here are some examples:

Backstory questions:

- Where are you from? Have you always lived there? Where did you grow up? Is that where your family is from?
- What is your name? How do you spell it? Am I saying it right? Does it have any meaning? What's your surname? Do you know any history of your family name? What about a middle name? Where does that come from?
- Do you have any siblings? What are they like? Are you close? What are they doing now?
- Are you more like your mum or your dad? What do they do? What are they like?
- What do you do? What did you do before that? How did you get into it? What do you like most about it? Is your team nice? How about your boss?
- What's the best holiday you went on as a kid? What's the best job you ever had? What's the best memory you have from growing up? What's the best thing that happened to you?
- What do you like to do in your free time?

Dreamy questions:

- If you could do any job, what would it be? If you didn't have to earn money, what would you do? When you were young, what was your fantasy job?

- If you could go anywhere in the world, where would you go? What would be your ideal holiday?
- What's your perfect Friday night? If you chose a famous person to hang out with, who would it be, and what would you do?
- If you could order any food as your last dinner, what would you choose?
- If you could learn anything, what would it be? If you had the time and the money, what hobby would you most like to take up?

You can see how all the questions start with something very safe and 'normal', and how they increase their depth over time. Please remember, though, this isn't an interrogation – conversations are reciprocal. You are allowed to share your responses to the questions too, it builds the trust necessary to get to the next level of depth.

When reading through the list of example questions, there are some that you would like to be asked, and some that you would find more challenging to answer. So be natural, go with the ones that make you feel comfortable – your comfort will come out in your body language and your tone and therefore make the other person feel more at ease.

Reflect & Write: Perhaps selecting from the list above, perhaps writing your own: next time you meet someone for the first time, what line of questions would you feel comfortable with?

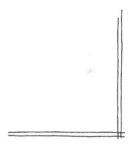

Conclusions

How to be interesting sounds like some dark art, and we're either born with a 'gift of the gab', or we're not. This isn't true – to be interesting, simply follow these five principles:

- Accept the fear of rejection is a natural human condition when entering a group.
- Manage your state sufficiently so that you can access a smile (and see *OWN LIFE WITH COURAGE* if you'd like some help in achieving this).
- Assume that everyone is wonderfully interesting once they feel comfortable enough to talk freely.
- Practise asking questions in a series that get increasingly deeper.
- Show appreciation by being curious and bringing your undivided attention.

CHAPTER 7
LISTENING

Whatever the topic, in this book, we have repeatedly underscored the importance of listening. Whether it's to deepen friendships, overcome conflict or be perceived as interesting, listening is the key, and it's not as straightforward as you perhaps imagined!

You may hear someone talking – that's the sound waves entering your ears – but listening requires your concentration too. You're only 'listening' when your brain is processing what it hears and makes meaning from the words and sentences (and the body language that accompanies them).

Behaviours of Listeners

I was at a party a while ago, the drinks had been flowing and while waiting to get served at the bar I was watching a group of four people chatting on the edge of the dancefloor. Because that was what they were all doing. All of them chatting, at the same time, to one another. All four mouths were moving non-stop, and it was pretty clear, even from a distance, that nobody was listening.

You have all experienced this at some time in your life, so let's not dwell on the obvious examples of bad listening, but instead notice the behaviours of the good listeners.

Reflect & Write: When you think of the good listeners in your life, what do they do well?

Reflect & Write: Sometimes you'll be a good listener, and at other times you don't listen so well. When you're not a good listener, what are you doing badly?

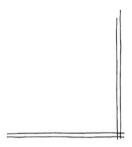

Bad Listening

You've noticed that you sometimes listen badly. Can you recognize some of these bad traits in yourself?

Distracted

You may not entirely ignore someone if they are talking directly with you, one-to-one. But you're ready to be distracted – by anything. Many years ago, when mobile phones were a novelty, I was having a chat with a colleague whose mobile phone rang. He answered it and proceeded to have a conversation with the caller while I stood like a lemon in front of him. Nowadays I have friends who think it is OK to pick up their phone and begin to browse through it while I'm talking to them. Do you know people who do this? Does your attention sometimes get pulled away from a conversation? Your behaviours make it clear that you are ignoring the other person.

Wandering

Have you ever been in a conversation with someone, and over time, as they continue to talk, your mind wanders? Has it ever wandered so far away that you completely forget the person is talking to you? You catch yourself and come back to the conversation with a jolt desperately trying to slip right back in again as though you've never been away. For the entire time the person is talking you've been on autopilot, and they know it because you've been saying 'uh-huh', and 'yeah', and 'uh-huh', and 'yeah', and 'uh-huh' and 'yeah', and when you come back from your mind wander you break the monotony by throwing in an 'exactly', or 'definitely', before returning to 'uh-huh', and 'yeah', and 'uh-huh', and 'yeah'.

Biased

Your mind is wandering, but you're also listening out for trigger words or phrases which will cause your full attention to come back to the talker. This is often the case when we're in conflict with the other person. While the other person is talking, we take the opportunity to give the brain time to construct our own next awesome point, while also keeping half an ear on their chatter in case something they say would be useful in our argument. In biased listening, you hear only the parts of the conversation that interest you.

Hijacking

You listen and hear all the words, and you relate to them by comparing what you hear with your life experiences. When the other person pauses, or when you interrupt them you take over (aka hijacking the conversation), based on your own frame of reference. You are likely to:

1. Evaluate: Agree or disagree with what is said.
2. Probe: Ask questions to satisfy your own needs.
3. Advise: Hand out unsolicited opinions on what should be done.
4. Interpret: Make meaning of what they are saying from your own point of view.

Most people listen with the intent to reply, not to understand. At any given moment, they're either speaking or preparing to speak. Next time you're in a conversation, notice where your attention is!

Good Listening
Thankfully, *7 Habits of Highly Effective People* author Stephen Covey[15] described a deeper level of listening, which he called 'empathetic listening'. He describes it as 'getting inside another person's frame of reference.'[16]

In this mode of listening the habits of judgement and preconceptions are silenced, and you've gone beyond being open-minded (where you're accepting that different world views exist). You're now in the realm of listening with an open heart. When you can do this, you connect with the other person not just on an intellectual basis, but on an emotional one too.

Remember the ladder of inference? If you're in bad listening mode, then you're inferring a lot about the other person. When you're employing Empathetic Listening, you're able to see each rung of the other person's ladder. They'll say, 'wow, you really get me!'. Now imagine if you 'get' everyone you work with, and everyone you live with, and everyone you hang out with. It doesn't mean you agree with them; it simply means that you know (not guess or assume) where they are coming from. And it feels great!

Reflect & Write: Who really 'gets' you? And how does it feel?

Being a Better Listener

We all have moments when we listen poorly, and even though we've now read some theory about it, we'll do it again. So instead of making a 'new promise' to ourselves never to do it, let's set an intention to create some conditions where we're less likely to fall into it unconsciously.

As a first step in the right direction next time someone comes to talk to you, stop whatever you are doing, put your phone away, turn your body to face the talker directly, and give them your full attention, or agree a time when you can. Don't multitask and listen. Just this evening, as I was writing this section of the book, my daughter burst into the room full of excitement to tell me about a funny YouTube video she'd just watched. My head was fully in writing the book and I didn't want to lose my flow, so I turned to her and said, 'I'd love to hear all about it, and listen to you properly, give me 15 minutes, and I'll come to your room.' And 15 minutes later she got my full, undivided attention.

Reflect & Write: Who do you often give half of your attention to, and what is it that typically distracts you? Choose five people who sometimes receive poor listening from you and make an intention to remove the distraction and give them your undivided attention.

To overcome biased listening, you need to develop a technique to help you to hear everything a person says rather than just those things that pass through your RAS filter. Have a go at summarising back what you have just heard. Use your own words but attempt to avoid adding your interpretation. Your goal is for the other person to say, 'yes, that's exactly what I was trying to say'.

A reminder – you're not agreeing with them or giving their argument greater weight, you're simply acknowledging that you understand where they're coming from. You may like to begin your summary with the words, 'Let me check that I fully understand your point of view and correct me if I don't get things exactly right, I'd really like to see how you see things.'

Reflect & Write: Whose ideas or thoughts do you dismiss without fully exploring their point of view?

At this level, there is a balance to be struck. Sometimes it is good to be active in a conversation – your probing and interpretation bring real depth of understanding. It's helpful. The question is about where your balance is. Can you stop yourself from doing it? Can you really bite your tongue and prevent yourself from hijacking the conversation and making it about yourself? Or perhaps you have the exact opposite challenge, maybe you lack the courage to bring your point of view into a conversation and are therefore hiding your contribution from others. Where do you sit on the scale?

TOO LITTLE
CONTRIBUTION

TOO MUCH
HIJACKING

Reflect & Write: In what situations should you be more mindful of your hijacking tendency, and what do you now intend to do differently? Or, when are you missing the opportunity to contribute?

Listen Like the Buddha

If you can imagine the Buddha sitting and listening to you talk, you begin to imagine what Empathetic Listening looks like in practice. I would like you to bring more 'open-hearted', Buddha-like listening to your relationships.

Reflect & Write: Who will you bring an open heart to more often, and therefore listen to fully and completely with no desire to hijack?

I love helping people to listen well. In fact, it's often the highlight of any programme I run. When I clearly define the roles of two people, person A is the talker, person B is the listener, then magic happens. Person A has space to fully say everything they want to say, and almost every time they say things out loud that bring new insights to themselves – because they are not going to be interrupted, their monologue meanders and arrives at destinations they never knew about.

For the listener, freeing them from any duty to do anything (no fixing, no need to prepare a response) brings complete relaxation and they are able to fully enjoy the experience of being with another person wholly, often for the first time in their life. By the end of it, a very common reaction is for the talker to say, "That was been amazing, thank you for helping me so much," to which the listener often responds, "But I didn't do anything." Of course they did do something – they did great listening, and it's perhaps one of the greatest 'doing' things that you can do for someone.

If there's one thing to take from this book that will enhance every relationship and therefore the quality of your life, it is to practice listening well at every opportunity.

CHAPTER 8
DEVELOPING POSITIVE RELATIONSHIPS

The quality of your relationships largely determines the quality of your life. It's entirely possible to grow the level of trust you experience as long as you take responsibility for making it happen. Follow these eight steps and you're sure to enjoy a wonderful life:

1. Water those relationships that bring you most emotional satisfaction.
2. Deepen the way you listen with an open heart.
3. Treat conflict as a requirement for seeing the world afresh.
4. Give well thought through feedback if you are hurt by others.
5. Readdress imbalance in relationships by seeking to hold the adult position.
6. Dive into the four dimensions of trust to build positive relationships.
7. Manage your internal state and crack a smile at every opportunity.
8. Honour the presence of other people by being fully present with them.

But let's not leave things right here. What you have now is an understanding of what you need to do. It's in your brain but it's not in your behaviours and we need to do something about that otherwise nothing really changes. We have to stimulate you into action and build momentum with a daily practice of intention and reflection. Over the next 30 days you're going to create a habit loop which places the development of positive relationships as a part of your daily life.

You're going to run tiny daily experiments, starting today and not skip a beat for an entire month. Here's the set of questions you'll be exploring with some guidance on each:

1. My experiment for today is to…
Take a look over the eight steps and choose one. Then define a simple, safe experiment you have the desire to undertake today. It should be something where the opportunity arises simply in the natural course of what's on your schedule for the day (rather than something that requires special planning). Feel free to repeat previous experiments, or run them again with tweaks – there's no need to come up with something entirely fresh every day.

2. I hope to learn…
You will naturally have a hypothesis about what you might learn from this experiment, so write it down. If your hypothesis is negative, change the experiment, don't design an experiment to prove bad things can happen!

3. What can I do to maximise the opportunity for the experiment to take place?
'I didn't have chance' may be a frequent reason why an intention didn't turn into action, so here you want to be

noticing anything that may cause the opportunity to pass by. If you're a procrastinator, then this step is crucial otherwise you'll forever find a convenient reason to 'start tomorrow'.

4. I learnt that...

You complete this after you've conducted the experiment. Notice the really intentional language I've used. We're calling this an experiment, and this section is about what you've learnt. No-where in this process is there a question asking – was it a success?

The goal of this process is to be really intentional about doing something to enhance your relationships, and to learn throughout the process. If you establish these two things as a habit then I guarantee you'll enjoy a better life.

I wish you every success in your journey ahead and trust you'll share it with many wonderful people.

Reflect & Write: Here follows your 30 days of My daily Experiments

1. My experiment for today is to…

2. I hope to learn…

3. What can I do to maximise the opportunity for the experiment to take place?

4. I learnt that…

1. My experiment for today is to…

2. I hope to learn…

3. What can I do to maximise the opportunity for the experiment to take place?

4. I learnt that…

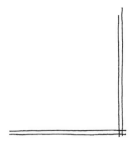

1. My experiment for today is to…

2. I hope to learn…

3. What can I do to maximise the opportunity for the experiment to take place?

4. I learnt that…

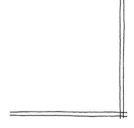

1. My experiment for today is to...

2. I hope to learn...

3. What can I do to maximise the opportunity for the experiment to take place?

4. I learnt that...

1. My experiment for today is to…

2. I hope to learn…

3. What can I do to maximise the opportunity for the experiment to take place?

4. I learnt that…

1. My experiment for today is to...

2. I hope to learn...

3. What can I do to maximise the opportunity for the experiment to take place?

4. I learnt that...

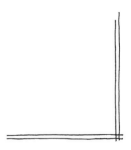

1. My experiment for today is to…

2. I hope to learn…

3. What can I do to maximise the opportunity for the experiment to take place?

4. I learnt that…

1. My experiment for today is to...

2. I hope to learn...

3. What can I do to maximise the opportunity for the experiment to take place?

4. I learnt that...

1. My experiment for today is to...

2. I hope to learn...

3. What can I do to maximise the opportunity for the experiment to take place?

4. I learnt that...

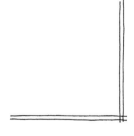

1. My experiment for today is to…

2. I hope to learn…

3. What can I do to maximise the opportunity for the experiment to take place?

4. I learnt that…

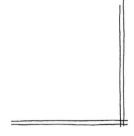

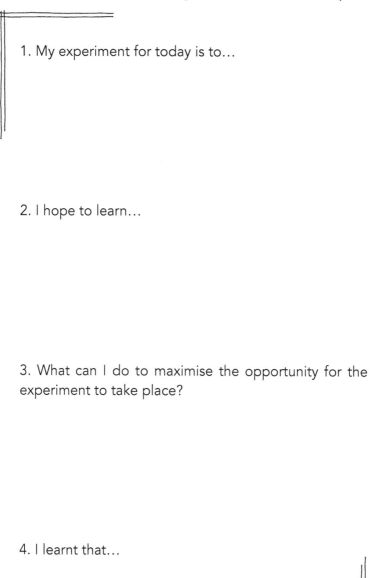

1. My experiment for today is to…

2. I hope to learn…

3. What can I do to maximise the opportunity for the experiment to take place?

4. I learnt that…

1. My experiment for today is to…

2. I hope to learn…

3. What can I do to maximise the opportunity for the experiment to take place?

4. I learnt that…

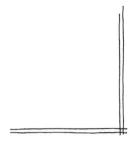

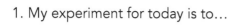

1. My experiment for today is to…

2. I hope to learn…

3. What can I do to maximise the opportunity for the experiment to take place?

4. I learnt that…

1. My experiment for today is to…

2. I hope to learn…

3. What can I do to maximise the opportunity for the experiment to take place?

4. I learnt that…

1. My experiment for today is to…

2. I hope to learn…

3. What can I do to maximise the opportunity for the experiment to take place?

4. I learnt that…

1. My experiment for today is to...

2. I hope to learn...

3. What can I do to maximise the opportunity for the experiment to take place?

4. I learnt that...

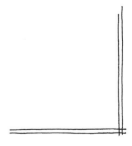

1. My experiment for today is to...

2. I hope to learn...

3. What can I do to maximise the opportunity for the experiment to take place?

4. I learnt that...

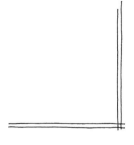

1. My experiment for today is to…

2. I hope to learn…

3. What can I do to maximise the opportunity for the experiment to take place?

4. I learnt that…

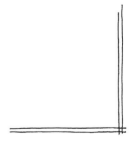

1. My experiment for today is to…

2. I hope to learn…

3. What can I do to maximise the opportunity for the experiment to take place?

4. I learnt that…

1. My experiment for today is to...

2. I hope to learn...

3. What can I do to maximise the opportunity for the experiment to take place?

4. I learnt that...

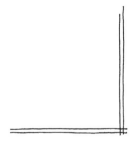

1. My experiment for today is to…

2. I hope to learn…

3. What can I do to maximise the opportunity for the experiment to take place?

4. I learnt that…

1. My experiment for today is to...

2. I hope to learn...

3. What can I do to maximise the opportunity for the experiment to take place?

4. I learnt that...

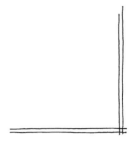

1. My experiment for today is to…

2. I hope to learn…

3. What can I do to maximise the opportunity for the experiment to take place?

4. I learnt that…

1. My experiment for today is to...

2. I hope to learn...

3. What can I do to maximise the opportunity for the experiment to take place?

4. I learnt that...

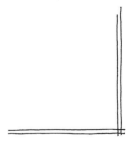

1. My experiment for today is to…

2. I hope to learn…

3. What can I do to maximise the opportunity for the experiment to take place?

4. I learnt that…

1. My experiment for today is to...

2. I hope to learn...

3. What can I do to maximise the opportunity for the experiment to take place?

4. I learnt that...

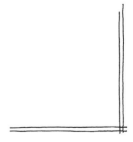

1. My experiment for today is to…

2. I hope to learn…

3. What can I do to maximise the opportunity for the experiment to take place?

4. I learnt that…

1. My experiment for today is to...

2. I hope to learn...

3. What can I do to maximise the opportunity for the experiment to take place?

4. I learnt that...

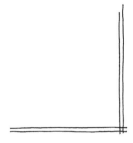

1. My experiment for today is to…

2. I hope to learn…

3. What can I do to maximise the opportunity for the experiment to take place?

4. I learnt that…

1. My experiment for today is to...

2. I hope to learn...

3. What can I do to maximise the opportunity for the experiment to take place?

4. I learnt that...

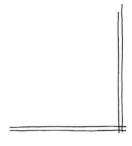

EPILOGUE
OWN ALL OF LIFE

HOW'S IT ALL GOING?

I asked you this question right at the start of the book. Let's pause again to step back from the details of life, and check-in. Well done for choosing to invest some time in yourself and pat yourself on the back for persevering to the end of the book – many of the self-reflection questions I posed are quite challenging.

Reflect and Write: Having worked through *OWN LIFE WITH TRUST* I will…

If you're ready to continue your OWN LIFE journey, where do you want to focus next?

OWN LIFE WITH CONFIDENCE:
How to grow into the best version of yourself
OWN LIFE WITH COURAGE:
How to thrive on the emotional rollercoaster of life
OWN LIFE WITH PURPOSE
How to engineer a lifestyle that fulfils your dreams

Congratulations on choosing to develop yourself. If this becomes a lifelong habit I guarantee you a wonderful life, and I wish you the very best of luck with it.

DEAR READER...

The very best thing about what I do is when I get to see people grow into their own skin and radiate a comfortable ease that only comes with being their wonderful authentic self. The magic is multiplied when I get to be a witness (and occasional mentor) as they continue their life journey. I would love to add you to the community of people I know who are actively working on improving themselves.

From time-to-time I share stories of my journey. The successes and the struggles. I also test new material and ask for guidance from my readers on what would be most helpful in the future. If you'd like to be a part of the Own Life community go to www.ownlife.me/connect

And... you can make a big difference to me right away.

Reviews are the most powerful way for an independent publisher like myself to help new readers find my books. And reviews are the most trusted source when new readers are choosing how to spend their money.

Honest reviews of my books help to nourish the entire system. If you've enjoyed this book, I would be super-appreciative if you could spend just five minutes leaving a review (which can be as brief as you like).

I really hope that I've been able to help you on your Own Life journey.

With big thanks,

todd@ownlife.me

ABOUT THE AUTHOR

Todd Eden's sole mission in life is to bring out the best in people. It wasn't always this way! Right through childhood and through his first couple of careers, he was insatiably competitive – great at bringing out his personal best and achieving results, but not always with great consideration for everyone around him.

Thankfully he married someone who simply oozes kindness. The resulting upgrade, Todd version 2.0, retains his authentic ambition to win at life but now defines winning as 'bringing out the best in others'.

This mission has taken him around the world working with multi-national companies; into the lecture theatres of a third of the UK's universities; and deep into the lives of his personal coaching clients.

He remains a passionate student of self-development and has been living and breathing it daily for decades. At live events he enjoys bringing his unique combination of profound life shifting moments with belly laugh humour to thousands of people. It's his wish that this book brings out the best in many thousands more.

Connect with Todd at www.ownlife.me/connect

ABOUT THE ILLUSTRATOR

From a young age, El Davo enjoyed art, and from seeing other people's reactions, he learned he had a talent. He attributes some of this to being curious and observational of his surroundings – or a daydreamer as others might put it. Those around him saw the need to nurture this talent well before he was aware of it himself.

He was lucky enough that his older sister was an artist, always there to offer invaluable support and encouragement when he was growing up. She lived in London at the time and regularly took him around the city to different galleries, as well as showing him all the graffiti and street art hotspots. Later she convinced him to pursue an art education beyond sixth form and attend art college, and after that, university.

Initially, he never felt like he'd earned this talent, but nonetheless felt obliged to make the most of it. He constantly strives to improve, for both the buzz of exceeding his own expectations and the joy it brings others. He especially loves to hear of people inspired enough to get back into doing art themselves. He firmly believes there's a huge pool of untapped creative talent in society, stuck inside people who haven't had the support and encouragement he's been fortunate enough to receive.

Connect with El Davo at www.eldavo.co.uk or on Instagram @eldavooo

"I believe in myself. I know and accept myself for exactly who I am today and feel inspired by how I will grow into the future."

[You, 6 months from now]

How to Grow Into the Best Version of Yourself

Accept yourself for who you are today, with all the beautiful flaws, without judgement

Clearly see a future enhanced version of yourself that is still authentically you

Overcome resistance to change and keep the development journey rolling

"My inner world is a positive place even when the outside world has its ups and downs. I'm resilient to setbacks and have found courage to push through fears that used to hold me back."

[You, 6 months from now]

How to Thrive on the Emotional Rollercoaster of Life

Create a separation between external events and internal emotions

Reprogram the filters through which you experience the world

Dare to do what you dream by pushing through fear

"I know where I'm heading in life and am grounded enough to enjoy each passing moment. I dream big, set plans, and make them happen. It's a thrill to be alive."
[You, 6 months from now]

How to Engineer
a Lifestyle that Fulfills your Dreams

Turn dreams, wishes and hopes into goals
that feel tinglingly possible

Give focus to your most precious priorities as
you become a blackbelt time master

Feel alive every day with energy
habits that boost resilience

"From making a good first impression to repairing age-old broken relationships; from deepening my most loving friendships to navigating conflict, I build trust with others."

[You, 6 months from now]

How to Develop Positive Relationships

Reframe your attitude to conflict through an enhanced desire to see new perspectives

Respond with calm maturity when triggered by the behaviour of others

Unleash the simple magic of listening with wholehearted attention

ENDNOTES

1   Carnegie, D. (2006) How to Win Friends and Influence People. London: Vermilion. Page 19

2   Boutin C. (2006) Snap judgments decide a face's character, psychologist finds. Princeton.edu. 22 August 2006. https://www.princeton.edu/news/2006/08/22/snap-judgments-decide-faces-character-psychologist-finds

3   If you would like to know a little more about Transaction Analysis, check out the summary here: http://www.ericberne.com/transactional-analysis/

4   Berne, E. (2010) The Games People Play. London: Penguin Books.

5   Argyris, C. (1990) Overcoming Organizational Defences: Facilitating Organizational Learning. New Jersey: Pearson Education.

6   Senge, P. (1990) The Fifth Discipline. Michigan: Doubleday/Currency.

7   Feltman, C. (2009) The Thin Book of Trust. Bend: Thin Book Publishing. Page 6.

8   Feltman, C. (2009) The Thin Book of Trust. Bend: Thin Book Publishing.

9   Lewis, R. (2014) How Different Cultures Understand Time. BusinessInsider.com. 01 June 2014. <https://www.businessinsider.com/how-different-cultures-understand-time-2014-5?r=US&IR=T>

10 Thanks to Jefferson Cann for this terminology

11 Warner, J (2012) Coaching Models: Johari Window. Blog. readytomanage.com. 20 March 2012.

12 Carnegie, D. (2006) How to Win Friends and Influence People. London: Vermilion. Page 56

13 Carnegie, D. (2006) How to Win Friends and Influence People. London: Vermilion. Page 96

14 Carnegie, D. (2006) How to Win Friends and Influence People. London: Vermilion. Page 91

15 Covey, S. (1989) The 7 Habits of Highly Effective People. London: Simon & Schuster. Page 236 to 260.

16 Covey, S. (1989) The 7 Habits of Highly Effective People. London: Simon & Schuster. Page 240.

INDEX